MW00584052

LIBRA

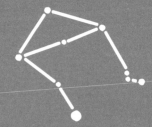

A GUIDED JOURNAL

Constance Stellas

ADAMS MEDIA
New York London Toronto Sydney New Delhi

Adams Media
An Imprint of Simon & Schuster, Inc.
100 Technology Center Drive
Stoughton, Massachusetts 02072

First Adams Media hardcover edition September 2022

ADAMS MEDIA and colophon are trademarks of Simon & Schuster.

For information about special discounts for bulk purchases, please contact Simon & Schuster Special Sales at 1-866-506-1949 or business@simonandschuster.com.

The Simon & Schuster Speakers Bureau can bring authors to your live event. For more information or to book an event contact the Simon & Schuster Speakers Bureau at 1-866-248-3049 or visit our website at www.simonspeakers.com.

Interior design by Colleen Cunningham
Interior illustrations by Tess Armstrong
Interior images © Getty Images/Vikiss, Mara Fribus; Simon & Schuster, Inc.

Manufactured in China

10 9 8 7 6 5 4 3 2 1

ISBN 978-1-5072-1953-9

CONTENTS

INTRODUCTION

Are you interested in how the stars may influence your characteristics? Wanting a little celestial insight into how you can strengthen your relationships? Looking for guidance in using your diplomatic talents to achieve your goals? Guided journaling can be a dialogue between your thoughts, feelings, and aspects of your sign and element. By reflecting in an intentional way, you can begin to understand yourself—and how you interact with the world around you—better.

An air sign, Libra is intelligent, communicative, and whimsical, but they can struggle with being decisive. Journaling can help you ground your ideas and make decisions you feel good about. Are there any relationships where your ideal and the reality of that person don't line up? Times when you've missed out on an opportunity because you couldn't make up your mind? The prompts in this book will allow you to choose with more confidence and translate your dreams to the real world by exploring your Libran tendencies and what you may share with other air signs.

Journaling can also help Libra find more balance. Libra's symbol is the scales, and Libra strives for harmony and fairness in all things. You can sometimes feel overwhelmed by harsh realities, conflict, and attempts to please everyone. Can you remember a time when you felt strong, even conflicting emotions but later discovered a middle way? By reflecting on the prompts in this book, you'll gain a deeper understanding of what has—and hasn't—helped you strike a balance and learn how to create a more harmonious future.

When you write, you connect with your feelings, desires, and everything in between. And when prompts drive you to contemplate the wealth of astrological wisdom that each element and Sun sign offers, it can lead to surprising, creative insights. Maybe you knew you loved beauty and symmetry but didn't realize how that love could be used to bring more relaxation and harmony into your living space. Or perhaps you had never considered the importance of open, uncluttered spaces as an air sign. This book will help you explore yourself and your place among the stars.

HOW TO USE THIS BOOK

Welcome to your astrology journal! This guided journal is divided into three parts to help you explore your connections to the stars.

PART ONE

First, there are prompts about astrology in general, from how you feel about astrological wisdom to what you notice about your relationships with different signs and your experiences with reading horoscopes. The long and rich history of astrology can truly enhance your life and deepen your self-knowledge. Whatever strikes your fancy is a prompt to pursue! The purpose is not to master celestial knowledge but to turn your thoughts to the cosmos and reflect in an intentional way that may uncover some surprising insights.

PART TWO

The second part features prompts about your element. In astrology, there are four elements:

- Fire
- Earth
- Air
- Water

There are three zodiac signs in each element.

THE
PASSIONATE
FIRE SIGNS
ARE:

ARIES   **LEO**   **SAGITTARIUS**

THE
PRACTICAL
EARTH SIGNS
ARE:

TAURUS   **VIRGO**   **CAPRICORN**

THE
COMMUNICATIVE
AIR SIGNS
ARE:

GEMINI   **LIBRA**   **AQUARIUS**

THE
EMOTIONAL
WATER SIGNS
ARE:

CANCER   **SCORPIO**   **PISCES**

All members of the same element have an affinity; being with your elemental brothers or sisters can often feel comfortable because they speak your language. Understanding the characteristics of your element can give insight into good health practices and ways to relax and recharge, as well as how you might approach aspects of life such as work and relationships.

PART THREE

Finally, the third part of this journal concentrates on your Sun sign. This is the position of the sun when you were born. The Sun sign is a dominant feature in a person's entire chart. It reveals your:

- Psychological characteristics
- Health habits
- Relationship affinities
- Spiritual mission in this lifetime

Each Sun sign also has a ruling planet that gives the sign a certain kind of energy; a symbol that represents the characteristics of the sign's personality; and a modality that reveals whether that sign charges ahead in life, prefers the security of things remaining the same, or is open to the changes that come along. Consider these prompts intuitively. When something speaks to you and you think "Yes! That's me," reflect on the questions and any suggestions posed by the prompt. If you don't feel particularly drawn to a prompt, you may want to return to it later. If the information or questions in a prompt make you feel uncomfortable, consider whether there is something hidden or suppressed in your life that it awakens. Or you may use the page to explore why this doesn't fit you. True, not every aspect of the Sun sign will resonate with every person, so you may want to look at your full birth chart to help color the portrait of you that you create in this journal.

Astrology has become more and more popular, thanks to the ease of calculating birth charts online; the availability of daily, weekly, or monthly horoscopes delivered straight to your inbox; popular lists of famous people according to their Sun signs; and more. Ancient astrologers may have appreciated these options, *but* a computer is not a person, and the information that computer printouts offer is standard. Anyone born on the same day, time, year, and place as you would have the same astrology chart; however, people are individuals. There's a lot more to you than what is written about a Sun sign or astrological element. The beauty of this journal is that you can reflect on what astrology means to *you* and understand the nuances of your sign and element and how they do or don't relate to you as a unique person. Use this journal as your guide in exploring what the stars can teach you about yourself!

Astrology is the study of star and planetary patterns and what they mean for individuals and societies. Observing the regular motions of the sun, the moon, and other planets, ancient people became adept at interpreting what these celestial bodies and cycles meant. Today, there is a new renaissance in astrology, thanks to the Internet. Now anyone can find out the locations of the sun, the moon, Venus, and more at the time of their birth in just seconds, and subscribe to a service featuring daily, weekly, and monthly astrological forecasts. Consulting astrologers also offer star wisdom for health, business dealings, romance, spiritual development, and marriage.

In this part, you'll find thought-provoking prompts to guide you in reflecting on astrology in a more general context, rather than focusing on one specific sign or element. The sun, the moon, Mercury, Venus, Mars, Jupiter, Saturn, Uranus, Neptune, and Pluto: All of these celestial energies make up a natal chart and become a blueprint for gaining deeper self-knowledge and guiding your life. You can explore the astrological patterns in your family, track how different events like eclipses and equinoxes impact your mood and experiences, consider your beliefs on fate versus free will, and more. Enjoy this journey into the cosmos.

PART ONE

GETTING TO KNOW THE WORLD OF ASTROLOGY

Imagine you are lying on the grass or a beach or sitting on a bench at night. You can see the stars, perhaps the moon. Depending on the time of year, you might even see Venus twinkling on the horizon or a distant red glow from Mars. Describe what you feel. Awe? Like you are part of the universe? Or like you are insignificant compared to the vast celestial sky? Maybe curious to know more about the heavens?

....
....
....
....
....
....
....
....
....
....
....
....
....
....
....
....
....
....
....
....
....

If you were an ancient navigator and only had the constellations and the moon with which to navigate your ship to get home, would you feel comforted by the regularity of the patterns in the night sky? Write about a time when you felt lost literally or emotionally. Did the moon or a twinkling star give you courage? Did you notice if the moon during that time was just a crescent or full? Or maybe it was somewhere in between?

Astrology has become more and more popular in recent years, thanks to the Internet! Do you believe that everything astrology says about your sign is true? Write about a positive experience you have had reading your horoscope. Did you follow the advice? What happened?

What charms you about astrology? What bothers or concerns you about it? Are you mindful of the monthly zodiac sign changes? Describe any feelings you have about how certain zodiac time periods affect you. For example, in spring, when the sun is in Aries, maybe you feel energized.

Are there certain signs with which you are more harmonious? Less harmonious? Write about your experiences.

A person's fate or destiny is a lifelong path. Describe how you feel when you read an astrological prediction for your future. Do you think it is good to know this information? Or better not to know? Do you use this information, keep it in mind, or ignore it?

Each zodiac sign is ruled by a planet or by the Sun or the Moon. Do you identify with Mercury, Venus, Mars, Jupiter, Saturn, Uranus, Neptune, Pluto, the Sun, or the Moon? Is it the planet your sign is ruled by? If not, describe your feelings about your own sign's planet. Do you think knowing more about your planet brings you insights into your personality or fortune?

The most famous—or infamous!—astrological event is Mercury Retrograde. This happens three times each year and means that Mercury appears to be moving backward in relation to the earth's orbit. It is common during these periods to experience electronic mishaps, communications going awry, and difficulties and delays in scheduling. Describe any Mercury Retrograde experiences you may have noticed. Were you forced to be more patient than usual?

If your Sun is in Gemini or Virgo, both signs ruled by Mercury, you may experience more personal confusion during Mercury in retrograde. Describe any personal confusion that you or your Gemini or Virgo friends experience at this time. Did you notice that you or they felt relief when Mercury was no longer retrograde?

....
....
....
....
....
....
....
....
....
....
....
....
....
....
....
....
....
....
....
....
....
....
....
....

....
....
....
....
....
....
....
....
....
....
....
....
....
....
....
....
....
....
....
....
....
....
....
....
....
....
....
....
....
....
....
....
....
....

The moon is our closest celestial neighbor, and its rhythms influence daily life. The monthly new moon marks the beginning of the moon's phases. At the new moon, people make wishes or set intentions with support from the moon's increasing energy as she waxes toward the full moon (the peak of lunar energy). Do you tend to notice the moon's phase, influence, or sign? Write about your relationship with and feeling toward this light.

Many astrologers believe that a person's chart can indicate past lives. What historical time period do you feel connected to? Who do you feel you might have been in a past life? What was your profession? Do you believe a past life can influence your present life? If so, how?

Each astrological sign is either masculine or feminine. This designation has nothing to do with gender or sexual orientation. The masculine signs radiate outwardly, and the feminine signs inwardly. Make a list of all the signs in your birth chart. Which energy dominates? Or perhaps they are equal? Do you feel these descriptions are true to your self-image?

In astrology, each sign has a symbol associated with it. Think about the symbol for your sign. Explore your feelings toward this symbol. Do any of its characteristics apply to you? You might write a story about yourself and what your symbol means to you. For example, as a Leo, are you more like a roaring lion or a purring cat?

....
....
....
....
....
....
....
....
....
....
....
....
....
....
....
....
....
....
....
....
....
....
....
....

As you will discover in this guided journey, there are four elements: fire, earth, air, and water. Each sign belongs to one element. Have you noticed that the signs of people you get along with have the same element as you do? Or a certain different element? Write about your experiences with people of the same and different elements.

Some people believe that following astrology curtails free will by forecasting the future. Do you believe this? Do you think it is possible that by knowing about your sign and using the stars as guides for the future you can make better choices in your life? Or do you feel controlled by what the stars say? Reflect on your feelings about free will and the stars.

Throughout the history of astrology, healers and physicians were required to study the positions of the planets in order to help their patients. They believed that the planetary energies could help or hinder healing the soul and body. What do you think about this idea? Can you implement any of your astrological insights into your health practices?

The position of the sun, the moon, and the ascendant are the three most important placements in a person's natal chart. If you know your birth time, you can easily determine these with the help of an app or astrology website. Explore your astrological trio and write down your feelings about these placements. Do you feel more connected to your moon or to your ascendant? Are there any patterns you notice, like the same element for each placement?

....

....

....

....

....

....

....

....

....

....

....

....

....

....

....

....

....

....

....

....

....

Eclipses were awesome phenomena for the ancients—and still have us in awe today! In a total solar eclipse, the sun's light is blocked by the moon, and the atmosphere darkens. In a lunar eclipse, the moon is blocked by the earth, and we cannot see this silvery orb. Most years have four eclipses. Do you pay attention to this heavenly event? Do you notice any patterns, either within yourself or in your surroundings during an eclipse? Research when the next eclipse will be, and record your feelings for the week leading up to the event.

How do you typically "use" astrology? Do you find it useful for self-understanding? Understanding other people? Exploring your friendships and/or partnerships? Do daily horoscopes guide your actions? Or do you see astrology as more of a guide for larger focuses in life? Write about an experience when an astrological tip helped you in some way.

Have you noticed that people in the same family often have the same signs? Or that other positions in their charts correspond? It's frequently the case! Take a look at your family's and extended family's signs, and reflect on the similarities and differences.

....
....
....
....
....
....
....
....
....
....
....
....
....
....
....
....
....
....
....
....
....
....
....
....
....

Saturn is the farthest planet you can see with the naked eye. It rules time, structure, and lessons of life. A major astrological transit is the Saturn Return, when Saturn returns to its natal chart position. This happens between ages twenty-eight and thirty. Where is Saturn in your chart? Have you experienced this return? Whether you have experienced your Saturn Return or not, write about your feelings toward the current path of your life, relationships, health, and spiritual development. If you have experienced your Saturn Return, how did your life look during these years?

Aside from your Saturn Return, another important transit (when a planet returns to its original position in your birth chart) is with the planet Jupiter. Jupiter is called the benefic of the zodiac. He helps us feel generous toward ourselves and others, is good for business, and can bring new areas of creativity into life. Jupiter returns to his birthplace every twelve years. Think about your birthday years at each twelfth year so far. Write about your feelings and activities in those years. Were the experiences positive? Expansive? Creative?

The solstices, summer and winter, occur at opposite signs: Cancer in the summer, and Capricorn in the winter. They mark the height of sunlight in summer and the depths of darkness in winter. How is your mood at these times? Describe how these essential astrological markers affect you.

Two major points in nature and the celestial calendar are the equinoxes: the fall equinox (Libra) and the spring equinox (Aries). These events mean there is equal daylight and darkness during that day. Do you have any particular feelings during these times of the year? Happy fall is coming after a hot summer? Or anticipating spring after a harsh winter? Write your feelings about the rhythm of nature and how it corresponds to your experience of the seasons. If you live in the southern hemisphere, the equinoxes are reversed.

If someone you know says, "I don't believe in astrology, it's rubbish," what do you say back? Write a dialogue between you and a skeptical person. What are your points of agreement? Of disagreement?

Have you ever noticed that some days feel lucky and positive and that during other days nothing seems to go right? It could be that the planetary pattern in the sky is not in harmony with your personal planets! Keep a record of good and bad days and the placements of the planets during each day. Reflect on any patterns. (You can find the daily position of the planets online.)

Throughout history, people have sought to understand the world around them. Today we have scientific equipment to inform us of the makeup of the universe, but ancient peoples could only observe the basic elements that they saw in their lives: fire, earth, air, and water. They associated each of these elements with an astrological sign and certain characteristics, and physicians used these characteristics to treat and heal their patients. The elements and their characteristics are:

FIRE (Aries, Leo, Sagittarius): Fire signs are known for their passionate energy and impetuosity. They often need to moderate their bursts of enthusiasm to prevent burnout.

EARTH (Taurus, Virgo, Capricorn): Earth signs are practical, cautious, and seek out security with a measured pace. Cultivating change and taking a few risks can enhance their lives, boost their health, and encourage flexibility.

AIR (Gemini, Libra, Aquarius): Air signs are changeable and mentally oriented; they enjoy living in creative possibilities and have highly sensitive nervous systems. Getting "down to earth" can help air signs move forward realistically.

WATER (Cancer, Scorpio, Pisces): Water is the element of feelings, and all water signs react to life emotionally. Calming their waves of emotion in order to see a situation clearly is a lifelong challenge for all water signs.

The more than two dozen prompts in this part of the book will give you a platform for understanding more about yourself and your nature based on your element.

PART TWO

GETTING TO KNOW YOUR ELEMENT

Many air signs have dreams about flying. Write about dreams when you were flying or suspended in air. What do you think these dreams mean? How do you feel when you wake up?

....
....
....
....
....
....
....
....
....
....
....
....
....
....
....
....
....
....
....
....
....
....
....
....
....

A common theme among air signs is shifting from one thing to the next and not giving enough time and focus to each of the different relationships and ideas and aspects of life. Consider your relationships and what is important in your life. Where might you want to devote more time to nourishing the things that already exist, versus coming up with new ideas or learning something new?

Imagine you are outdoors in the country or at the seashore and the wind begins to blow strongly. How do you feel? Do you stay outside? Find shelter? Do you feel energized, nervous, or curious? Write about an experience where the wind or quality of the air played a major part.

Stumped by a problem or difficult decision? Air signs have so many thoughts that they can struggle with indecision. An ancient oracle practice says that if you go into the marketplace (a mall will do just as well!) and note the first snatch of conversation you overhear, you may find the answer to your dilemma. Try it, and record your experience.

....

....

....

....

....

....

....

....

....

....

....

....

....

....

....

....

....

....

....

....

....

....

....

Air signs are creative idea people. They build "castles in the air," whether or not the castles are doable or practical. Air is also the element of communication. Imagination is nothing if an air sign can't share and communicate their ideas. Flex your communication muscles by describing a time when you imagined a wonderful idea that you worked hard to make come true.

....
....
....
....
....
....
....
....
....
....
....
....
....
....
....
....
....
....
....
....
....
....
....

Do you prefer to live up high in the mountains? Or in a skyscraper in the city? Or maybe an attic in your home? Is having a view and lots of windows important to you? Air signs often choose places where they can feel close to the sky, or at least have a great view of it. Describe your ideal living environment.

Air signs are known for their thinking ability and the way they communicate. They love to tell stories. Consider how often you begin a story or conversation with "I think" rather than "I feel." Has there been a time when what you thought and what you felt were in contrast? What happened?

Air quality is important to air signs particularly. You may notice you feel lethargic or weighed down when there are too many particles or ozone in the air. Strike back! Research the many organizations that promote clean air to find out what you can do to help the air quality in your home and region. Write about what you learn in your research and your experiences with the organizations you look into.

Activities that involve being in the air, such as hot air balloon rides, are perfect for air signs. Imagine that you are taking a hot air balloon ride on a perfect sunny day. Are you thrilled? Scared? What do you see below you? Write about what you imagine your reaction would be and what you think about the experience. If you have actually taken a balloon ride, describe your feelings both during that experience and now. Air signs have a talent for considering different perspectives. Did taking the ride change your perspective on anything?

Air signs are particularly sensitive to mental overstimulation. Have you ever had rushing thoughts that were a challenge to quiet? During these moments, you may have difficulty focusing and your breathing becomes shallow or panicky. Describe these experiences and how you were eventually able to quiet your thoughts. If you weren't able to quiet them, what might you try in the future to make it easier? Is there a breathing exercise or meditation practice you've heard about but never got around to?

....
....
....
....
....
....
....
....
....
....
....
....
....
....
....
....
....
....
....
....
....

Air signs are often talented in speaking foreign languages. Their quick minds can translate one language to another. Does this apply to you? If so, write about the languages you know and how they give a different mood or more depth to your communication. If you have never spoken a different language, what language would intrigue you to learn?

....
....
....
....
....
....
....
....
....
....
....
....
....
....
....
....
....
....
....
....
....
....

Vitamin O, meaning oxygen, is the most important part of an air sign's physical and mental health. Describe a time when just walking outside for a bit, opening a window, or standing out on a porch or balcony cleared your mind, boosted your breathing, and gave you a fresh view.

....
....
....
....
....
....
....
....
....
....
....
....
....
....
....
....
....
....
....
....
....
....
....
....

Multitasking was made for air signs! But if you find random thoughts or a long to-do list interfering with your ability to concentrate fully on one thing, your agile mind may need a little discipline. Write about a time when you had to concentrate on a task and kept interrupting yourself. How did you get focused? Or how did the lack of concentration affect the end result?

Wind chimes, mobiles, and prayer flags that flutter in the wind are perfect decorative items for air signs. Do you like these airborne pieces of art? Do they relax your mind? Give you inspiration?

....

....

....

....

....

....

....

....

....

....

....

....

....

....

....

....

....

....

....

....

....

....

....

....

....

....

....

Boredom is the enemy of air signs! Your mind is so quick and your curiosity so strong that repetitive tasks or tedious conversations can drain your energy. What do you do when you are bored? Describe a boring encounter or experience and how you relieved the situation.

....
....
....
....
....
....
....
....
....
....
....
....
....
....
....
....
....
....
....
....
....
....
....
....
....

The air element is the most elusive element of the zodiac. Write down all the expressions you know about air (e.g., "hold my breath," "left me breathless," "air dirty laundry," "walking on air"). Do any of these phrases remind you of a certain story or experience that is meaningful to you?

One myth from ancient Greece tells the story of Icarus, a young boy who, while trying to escape a labyrinth, took the wings his father had made and flew off. His father warned him not to fly too close to the sun, but Icarus didn't listen, and the wings melted, sending him into the sea below. Icarus followed his idea and desire rather than good sense. Think about a time when you ignored your own good sense in favor of an idea or desire. What happened?

Air signs love picnics, dining al fresco, and sitting in outside dining rooms. Describe your experiences with eating in the open air. How are they different from your experiences with indoor dining?

Writing is a particularly favorite air element activity! Air signs often feel compelled to write down their thoughts. Describe your feelings about writing. Do you feel relieved when you get something down on paper? Have you ever taken a class or longer course in writing?

Air signs like to travel because seeing new places stimulates ideas. Imagine you could take a ride on a magic carpet to anywhere you like. Would you go to a familiar place? Or maybe a scene from a fairy tale? Or to outer space? Write your thoughts about places that intrigue you and what you would do there.

As an air sign, your love of communication can boomerang if you are listening to or talking with negative people or about negative subjects. You appreciate the meanings of words, and when people throw around angry, cynical, or hurtful words, it affects you. Write about a time when you had to stop such a conversation or walk away from it. Even with this negativity problem, have you remained friendly with the person?

Air signs are so witty and quick with conversation that sometimes they speak without thinking. Have you had this experience? What happened? Did your words unintentionally hurt someone's feelings? What about a time when you kept your mouth shut to avoid the possibility of insulting someone?

When you take a walk in the woods or a garden, do you notice the leaves of the trees or plants blowing in the wind? Get in touch with your element by imagining a conversation with the wind, in which it sends you messages and creative ideas.

Air signs love to share jokes—and often have a talent for telling them! What is the funniest joke you have ever heard or come up with? Describe the laughter as you heard or told that joke.

Air signs can be unpredictable because they spend their time thinking up big ideas and concepts. Do you enjoy flexibility and spontaneity? Write about a time when you went in an unplanned direction, and everything worked out. Then reflect on the opposite situation: When did following a great idea end up being problematic? How?

The most important area of the body for air signs is the lungs. Healthy lungs support the rest of your physical system. Write down any difficulties, such as asthma or bronchitis, you have had. How did these make you feel? If you don't have difficulties with your lungs, write about how intentionally breathing deeply benefits your health.

....

....

....

....

....

....

....

....

....

....

....

....

....

....

....

....

....

....

....

....

....

....

The twelve astrological signs we know today come from the twelve constellations arranged around the ecliptic of the sun's path. Astrologers observe these signs and interpret their effect on people and events. For example, an astrologer may note that as a Virgo, a person might be great at analysis but find it challenging to synthesize all the details. And a Scorpio may be drawn to jobs or a certain career where they can investigate people or subjects, but a corporate structure doesn't appeal to them. Through understanding your Sun sign, you have a unique window of insight into yourself and your life!

The prompts in this part will guide you through a deeper exploration of your Sun sign and the traits, relationship dynamics, and more that may be influenced by this sign. Reflect on how your career path may be impacted by your sign. Consider how a certain characteristic linked to your sign plays into how you handle conflict with friends. Through guided journaling, this part will help you get to know yourself better. Of course, there is much more to astrology than your personal Sun sign. If you are interested in knowing even more about your relationship with the cosmos, you can also look at the other signs in your birth chart, such as your ascendant sign. Or you may want to focus more deeply on general astrology, as well as your Sun sign and sign element, and revisit different prompts to see how your reflections may evolve. This is *your* astrological journey: Let it take you wherever you want to go!

PART THREE

GETTING TO KNOW YOUR SIGN

Libra is known for their ability to consider all sides of a question and listen to all opinions before they make a decision. But sometimes this quality leads to indecision, confusion, and overwhelmed feelings. Write about a time that you missed out on an opportunity because you couldn't make up your mind.

Libra is ruled by Venus, the goddess of love and beauty. Write about a time when your love of beauty led you to a person you were attracted to. Is this a romance that may bring about a deep partnership or fun, more casual flirting? Both are possible for Librans, and it is good to know the difference. Describe the way you met and what you hope for the future of the relationship.

A statue frequently seen in front of courthouses is called Blind Justice; it depicts a blindfolded woman holding the scales of justice. She is blindfolded because justice is fair and impartial. The same scales are the symbol for your zodiac sign, Libra! Write about a time when you fought for or showed justice to someone or a certain cause.

Do you feel that Libra is an introverted or extroverted sign?
Describe a time when you felt you had both qualities. What are the
situations that bring out your introverted side? And those where
you feel extroverted? When you need to recharge, do you like to be
alone or with other people?

Libra can go to extremes to please a partner and keep a relationship. If you have had this experience, describe how you tried—or are trying—to find more balance between your needs, your desire to please, and your partner's needs. Is there a practice that always works for you to rein in the extremes?

Each zodiac sign has a challenging or "shadow" side. This is the part of your personality that you feel gets you into difficulties or that you may try to hide out of guilt or shame. Describe what you feel is your Libra shadow or "downside." Has this aspect changed as you have grown over time? Write about a time when you got around or worked with your shadow side. Also write about a time when you felt unable to get out of your own way.

Libra, loving romance, sets great store by giving and receiving gifts. What is the most romantic or meaningful present you have ever received? Who gave it to you, and what did it mean to you? Do you still have it?

....
....
....
....
....
....
....
....
....
....
....
....
....
....
....
....
....
....
....
....
....
....
....
....

The quest for balance is a lifelong pursuit for Librans. Have you experienced extreme feelings in a situation where you eventually found a harmonious resolution? Who was involved, and how did you achieve balance?

....
....
....
....
....
....
....
....
....
....
....
....
....
....
....
....
....
....
....
....
....
....
....
....

Librans usually prefer to stay away from conflict. But while anger can sometimes keep you stuck in negativity; it can also motivate you to make a valuable change. Describe a time when you were truly angry. What was the result? Were you able to let that anger go after the conflict?

Color is all-important to artistic Libra! Which are your favorite colors? Are they pastels? Shades of a primary color? Do you have a lucky color? Write about a time when the colors you wore helped make an experience memorable.

Clearing clutter can be a way to clear emotional as well as material stuff. Libra does best in open, airy spaces without chaos. Write about a time when you cleared out a room or closet. How did you feel afterward?

....
....
....
....
....
....
....
....
....
....
....
....
....
....
....
....
....
....
....
....
....
....
....
....
....

Love of luxury is a Libra hallmark. Describe a time when you indulged in something luxurious. What was it? Silk pajamas? Silk scarves? (Libra rules silk.) Or maybe your favorite luxury is jewelry; your birthstone, opal, is beautiful.

For Libra, sleep really is the best medicine! It restores balance. But Libra also likes parties and socializing, which can interfere with a good night's sleep. Do you have a nightly ritual for going to sleep? Write about a time when you were socially exhausted and couldn't get to sleep. What did you do? How do you feel on days following poor sleep? Edgy? Cranky?

....
....
....
....
....
....
....
....
....
....
....
....
....
....
....
....
....
....
....
....
....
....

Libra is known to be high-strung. A good nighttime ritual for you would be to imagine yourself in a warm bath with candles all around. This ritual can soothe all the accumulated experiences of the day. Write about this or other ways you have found to calm your nerves.

The sign Libra is halfway between the beginning of the zodiac and the end of the zodiac. Libra's purpose is to balance the personal development of an individual within the larger, impersonal development of society. Describe a time when you felt conflict between what you needed and what society was offering. This could be through a job, a relationship, or an education.

Librans may idealize love and compare their partner to an image they have of romance. Usually, a real partner cannot measure up, and this brings about frustration and conflict. At the same time, Libra thrives on relationships, and severing ties feels unnatural to them. Describe a relationship where how you felt (or currently feel) about a romantic partner, friend, or coworker contrasts with how you believed (or currently believe) the relationship "should" be. Are you being realistic?

Libra frequently pays people compliments: "You look great." "Love your hair!" "Ooh, that jacket is beautiful." Think about a time when you felt complimentary toward someone's internal qualities. For example, the way they handled their children or a sticky situation at work. You might notice that what you admired is a quality you value in yourself.

How do the people in your social circle describe you? What do they feel are your best characteristics? What are the habits that may irritate them? You can conduct a survey of their thoughts, or imagine how they would answer these questions. What do you agree with, and what do you feel is off base?

Libra is the sign of relationships and partnerships. If you were to describe the single most important relationship experience (positive or negative) of your life, what would it be? How has it impacted your life?

....
....
....
....
....
....
....
....
....
....
....
....
....
....
....
....
....
....
....
....
....
....
....
....
....

Libra enjoys soothing sounds and songs about love. What is your favorite kind of music? Write about an experience when listening to music or catching a song on the radio or in a store brought you back to a certain memory. What was the memory?

Venus rules Libra. In ancient times, Venus was the goddess of love and beauty. She was also a charmer who could persuade people into less-than-favorable situations. Do you recognize either of these archetypes in yourself? Write about a time when the goddess of love may have battled with the charmer in your life.

....

....

....

....

....

....

....

....

....

....

....

....

....

....

....

....

....

....

....

....

....

....

....

Libra has a very sensitive nervous system. Think about a time when you felt nervous. What was happening? Were there other people involved? How did you calm down?

Although a cardinal leadership sign, in general, Libra is not keen on leading aggressive sports. What is your favorite sport? Do you like team sports? Solo athletics? What do you find interesting or beautiful about these activities?

Sweets, sweets, and more sweets can be a Libran downfall. If this describes you, how do you moderate your cravings? Which sweet is your go-to? Write about an experience with sweets, using as many of the five senses as you can. Also reflect on any tricks you use to avoid overindulging.

....
....
....
....
....
....
....
....
....
....
....
....
....
....
....
....
....
....
....
....
....
....
....
....

Libra is the sign of partnerships. List words that describe your ideal partners in business, love, and friendship. Which are most important to you? Try to narrow it down to the top three and consider who you know that fits this description.

If you decide to travel, Libra, would you most enjoy camping, a cruise, a luxury hotel, or staying with friends? How does your choice reflect the essence of your sign?

ADDITIONAL RESOURCES

Websites and Other Digital Resources

www.alabe.com

www.astro.com

www.astrodienst.com

www.lunarium.co.uk

www.changingofthegods.com

App: Co-Star

Books

Astrology, Psychology and the Four Elements by Stephen Arroyo

The Astrology of Fate by Liz Greene

Sun Signs by Linda Goodman

Relationship Signs by Linda Goodman

If You Want to Write by Brenda Ueland

The Artist's Way by Julia Cameron

The Hidden Life of Trees by Peter Wohlleben

The Hidden Power of Everyday Things by Constance Stellas, Julie Gillentine, and Jonathan Sharp

Sex Signs by Constance Stellas

The Astrological Guide to Self-Care by Constance Stellas

How to Be an Astrologer by Constance Stellas

The Little Book of Self-Care by Constance Stellas

BIBLIOGRAPHY

Arroyo, Stephen. *Astrology, Psychology and the Four Elements.* Davis, CA: CRCS, 1975.

Arroyo, Stephen. *Relationships & Life Cycles.* Vancouver, WA: CRCS, 1979.

Donath, Emma Belle. *Have We Met Before?* Tempe, AZ: American Federation of Astrologers, 1982.

Forrest, Steven. *The Book of Neptune.* Borrego Springs, CA: Seven Paws, 2016.

Forrest, Steven. *The Book of Fire.* Borrego Springs, CA: Seven Paws, 2019.

Green, Jeffrey Wolf. *Pluto: The Evolutionary Journey of the Soul, Volume I.* St. Paul, MN: Llewellyn, 1985.

Green, Jeffrey Wolf. *Pluto: The Soul's Evolution Through Relationships, Volume II.* St. Paul, MN: Llewellyn, 1997.

Greene, Liz. *The Astrology of Fate.* York Beach, ME: Weiser, 1984.

Hickey, Isabel M. *Astrology: A Cosmic Science.* Sebastopol, CA: CRCS, 2011.

Oken, Alan. *Soul Centered Astrology.* New York: Bantam, 1990.

Sargent, Lois Haines. *How to Handle Your Human Relations.* Tempe, AZ: American Federation of Astrologers, 1958.

Tester, Jim. *A History of Western Astrology.* New York: Ballantine, 1987.

Yott, Donald H. *Astrology and Reincarnation.* York Beach, ME: Weiser, 1989.

DEDICATION

To all those seeking the wisdom in their stars.

ACKNOWLEDGMENTS

I would like to thank Karen Cooper and everyone at Adams Media who helped with this book. To Brendan O'Neill, Katie Corcoran Lytle, Laura Daly, Julia Jacques, Sarah Doughty, Jo-Anne Duhamel, Julia DeGraf, and everyone else who worked on the manuscripts. To Frank Rivera, Priscilla Yuen, Colleen Cunningham, and Tess Armstrong for their work on the book's cover and interior design. I appreciated your team spirit and eagerness to dive into the riches of astrology.

Unique ways to refresh and restore— personalized for your

ZODIAC SIGN!

  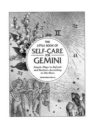 

PICK UP OR DOWNLOAD YOUR COPIES TODAY!